Contents

LittleBrother
BOOKS

Published 2018.
Little Brother Books Ltd, Ground Floor,
23 Southernhay East, Exeter, Devon, EX1 1QL
books@littlebrotherbooks.co.uk
www.littlebrotherbooks.co.uk
Printed In Poland

The Little Brother Books trademark, email and website addresses,
are the sole and exclusive properties of Little Brother Books Limited.
Images used under license from PA Images and Shutterstock.com.

Little Mix
and You!

Here's your chance to scribble all about you, plus what you like about the best pop group on the planet!

My name:

My age:

My BFF:

My fave Little Mix star:

She's my fave because:

My fave Little Mix song:

My fave Little Mix album:

3 things I love about Little Mix:

1.

2.

3.

Little Mix's Big Journey

Discover how the girls went from unknown artists to the UK's most successful girl band this century!

2011

Jade, Jesy, Perrie and Leigh-Anne appear at *The X Factor* auditions – as individual singers and not a group.

They reach the Boot Camp stage of the TV show, but the judges are not totally blown away by their solo singing.

Eventually the girls are put together in a group. The fantastic foursome performs brilliantly!

In December, Little Mix become the first group to win *The X Factor* and are loved by the judges, voters and the nation.

Little Mix's first song, *Cannonball*, flies straight into number 1 on the charts.

2012

Fans have to wait several months until the band's next single, called *Wings*, is released in September. Luckily it's a belting track and goes to number 1 and spends 25 weeks in the charts!

The band's amazing first album, *DNA*, is also available in time for Christmas. It's the perfect prezzie for lovers of Little Mix!

2013

It's another busy year for Jesy, Perrie, Jade and Leigh-Anne. They appear on US radio shows and websites as their international fame explodes. In the UK, singles *Move* and *Little Me* are released from their second album, called *Salute*.

2014

The title track *Salute* is released from Little Mix's second album. The band also has their first UK arena tour, playing at huge venues in London, Cardiff, Glasgow, Birmingham, Manchester and many more.

2015

The year, *Black Magic* conjures up lots of records for Little Mix! It becomes their biggest single so far, spending three weeks at number 1 and a mega 41 in the charts. The band puts out four other songs in 2015, including *Hair* and *Love Me Like You*.

Get Weird is Little Mix's third album. Fans love its funky grown-up sounds and it shoots to number 2 in the album charts.

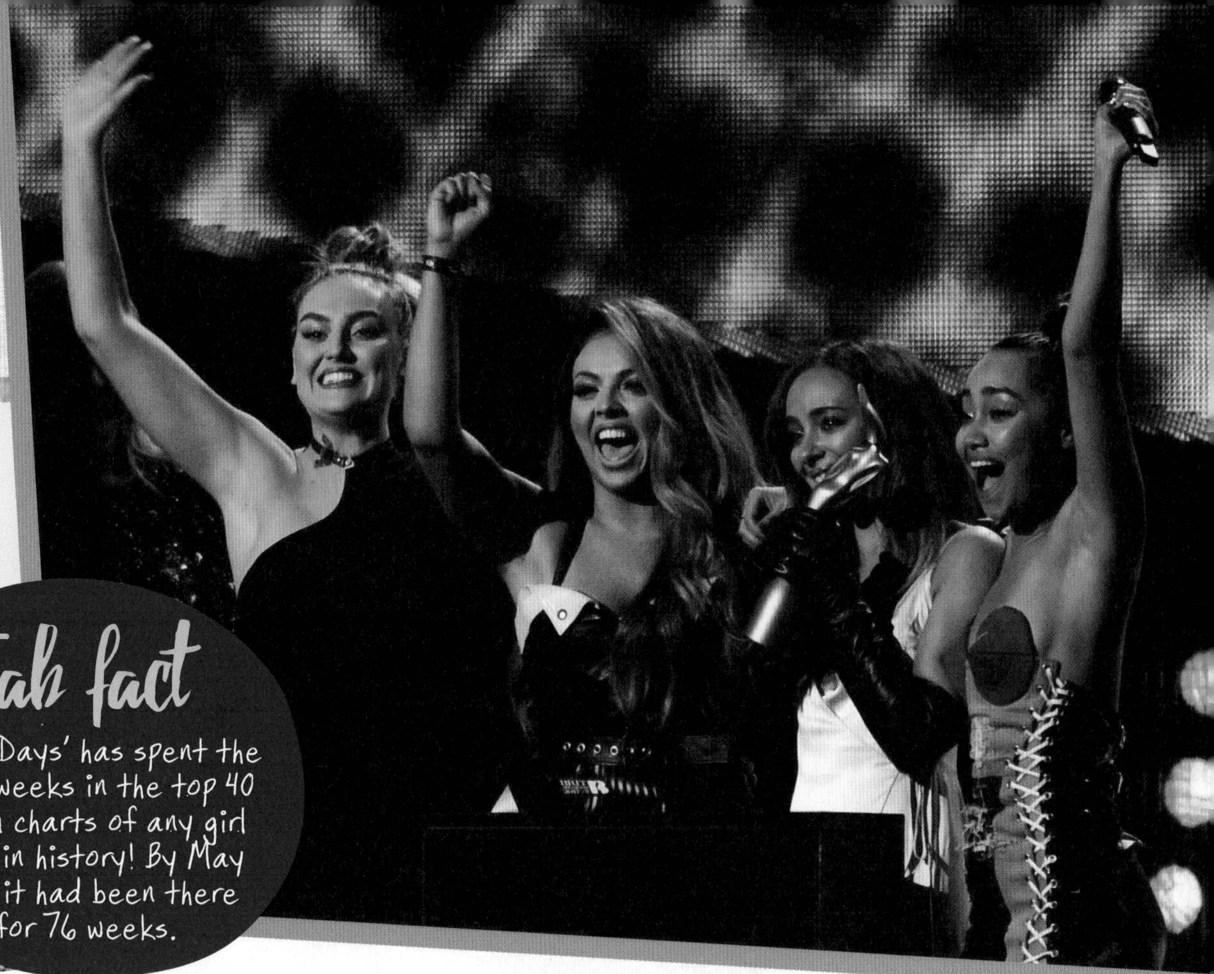

Fab fact

'Glory Days' has spent the most weeks in the top 40 album charts of any girl band in history! By May 2018 it had been there for 76 weeks.

2016

In 2016, Little Mix finally secure their first number 1 album! *Glory Days* is the foursome's best yet and is eventually knocked off top spot after five weeks.

When the song *Shout Out To My Ex* storms to number 1 in October, Little Mix become the first X Factor winners to have four chart-topping singles. Massive congrats, girls!

2017

It's award time. The band scoops their first Brit Award when *Shout Out to my Ex* is voted Best British Single.

The group also supports pop queen Ariana Grande on her *Dangerous Woman* tour in America. *The Glory Days* tour kicks off in May and is so popular that ten extra dates are added in the UK.

2018

Leigh-Anne reveals the brilliant news that in March, Little Mix will start writing songs for their fifth album. "We love inspiring people with our music. That's what we do," she says.

2019 ?

You can probably expect the band to go on tour again, performing songs from their new album. The Little Mixers can't wait to see them!

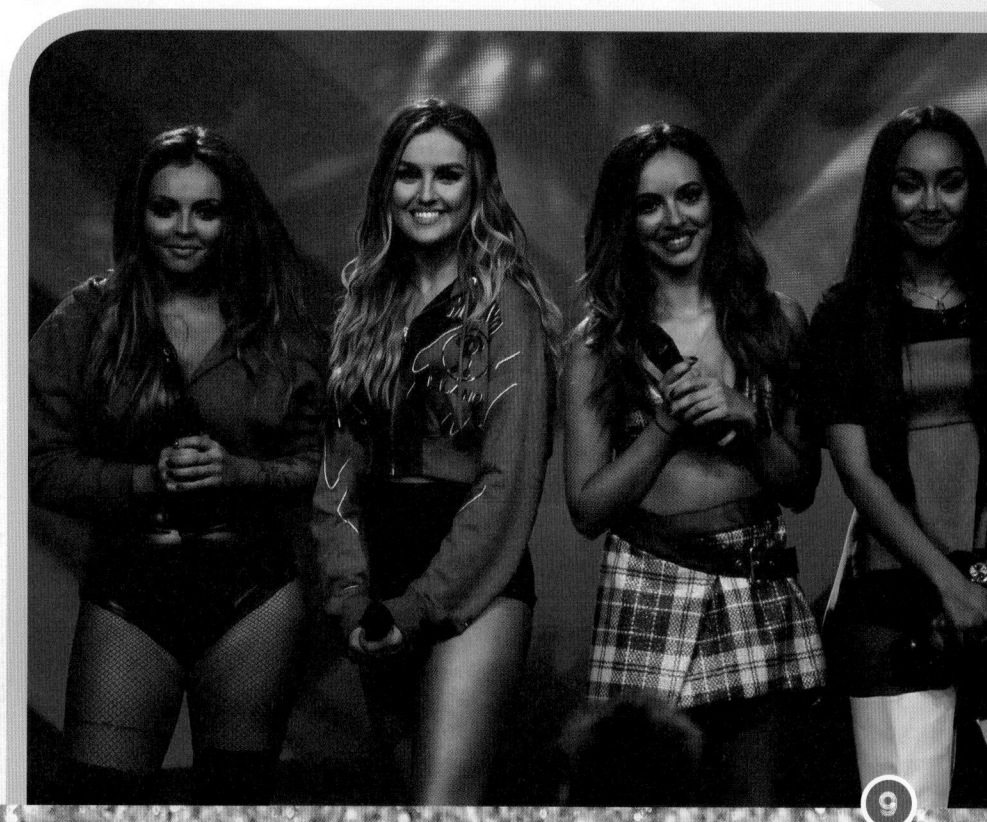

all about

Jesy

NAME:
Jessica Louise Nelson

NICKNAME:
Jesminda

FROM:
Romford, Essex

INSTAGRAM FOLLOWERS:
3.8 million

MUSIC HEROES:
Beyoncé and Missy Elliot

BIRTHDAY:
14th June, 1991

FAVE COLOURS:
Black and red

STAR SIGN:
Gemini

STYLE ICON:
Gwen Steffani

Fab fact

Jesy went to the famous Sylvia Young Theatre School and Rita Ora was in her class!

all about Jade

NAME:
Jade Amelia Thirlwall

NICKNAME:
Poopey

FROM:
South Shields,
Tyneside

INSTAGRAM FOLLOWERS:
4.4 million

MUSIC HEROES:
Beyoncé and Amy
Winehouse

BIRTHDAY
26th December,
1992

FAVE COLOURS:
Teal and purple

STAR SIGN:
Capricorn

STYLE ICON:
Alexa Chung

Fab fact

Jade's school friends called her 'Pickle'. They thought she was so small she could fit in a pickle jar!

all about

Leigh-Anne

NAME:
Leigh-Anne
Pinnock

NICKNAME:
Leigh-Leigh

**INSTAGRAM
FOLLOWERS:**
3.6 million

BIRTHDAY
4th October, 1991

STAR SIGN:
Libra

FROM:
High Wycombe,
Buckinghamshire

MUSIC HEROES:
Mariah Carey and
Michael Jackson

FAVE COLOUR:
Green

STYLE ICON:
Rihanna

Fab fact

Before she was famous, Leigh-Anne worked as a waitress at Pizza Hut.

all about

Perrie

NAME:
Perrie Louise
Edwards

NICKNAME:
Pez

INSTAGRAM
FOLLOWERS:
7.9 million

BIRTHDAY:
10th July, 1993

STAR SIGN:
Cancer

FROM:
South Shields,
Tyneside

MUSIC HEROES:
Beyoncé and
Steve Perry from
Journey

FAVE COLOUR:
Blue

STYLE ICONS:
Ashley Olsen &
Mary-Kate Olsen

Fab fact

Perrie was born in England but lived in New Zealand for two years from the age of 11.

guess who?

Jot down the name, or names, to answer each question.

1 Who is the oldest member of the group?

2 Who is the youngest?

3 Which two have the middle name Louise?

4 Who has the most instagram followers?

5 Who has a dog called Harvey?

6 Who used to live in New Zealand?

7 Who once worked as a waitress in Pizza Hut?

8 Who loves eating biscuits the most?

9 Who would like to sky dive from a plane?

Little Mixed-Up

The Little Mix superstars are all mixed up! Are you able to put all the girls back together for their next music award ceremony?

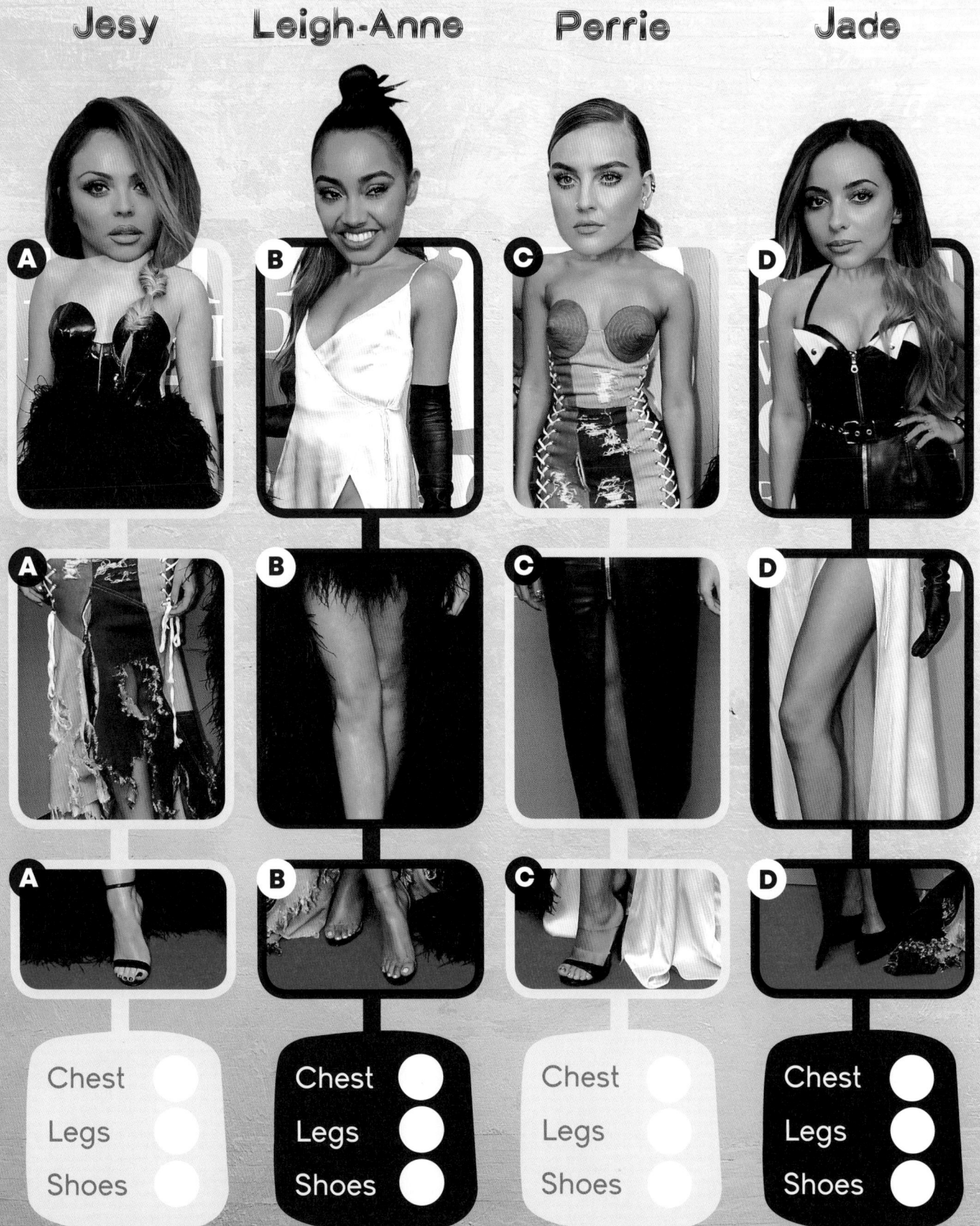

Jesy   Leigh-Anne   Perrie   Jade

	Jesy	Leigh-Anne	Perrie	Jade
Head	A	B	C	D
Body	A	B	C	D
Legs	A	B	C	D
Shoes	A	B	C	D

Chest ○
Legs ○
Shoes ○

Chest ○
Legs ○
Shoes ○

Chest ○
Legs ○
Shoes ○

Chest ○
Legs ○
Shoes ○

ANSWERS ON PAGE 76-77

19

Which Little Mix are you like?

I'm known for being late and struggling to keep on time!

I would sleep all day if I could. Zzzz!

Out of my friends, I hog the mirror the most.

I enjoy spicy Indian food. Yum!

I'm the clumsy one in my group of friends.

I love eating biscuits. Yum, yum!

I get upset watching sad films.

I'm probably the quiet one among my mates.

Making my hair look amazing is important to me.

See which of the pop princesses you're most like. Tick the four sentences that best describe you!

I say silly and fun things to my friends.

My favourite Disney princess is Jasmine.

I'd love to make a big movie with my friends.

Mostly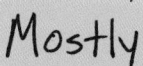
You and Perrie could be bezzies! You're a little bit crazy, but lots of fun... when you're not having sleepy lie-ins!

Mostly ◆
You're very similar to Leigh-Anne. You can be clumsy, but your friends love your caring ways. Don't forget to wear your watch, though!

Mostly ★
Like Jesy, you always wanted to be a big star. You look fantastic every day and have more hair care products than all of your friends!

Mostly ♥
You may often be quiet but, just like Jade, you have lots of energy and fun – especially after a chocolate digestive!

The little Mix Look

The girls are fab fashion icons! From sleek dresses to sporty gear and street style, Little Mix always look incredible.

Little Mix have lots of styles. Here, Jade captures the geek chic look with a classic tee and wide braces.

On stage, the group mixes it up with bright colours. These red, white and black outfits are super cool!

Jesy teams a black leather skirt with an elegant top. She rocks the celebrity red carpet looking like this!

Perrie pulls off this striking blue belt/cropped skirt piece with total ease. It's unusual but amazing!

Jesy also loves a bit of rock chick. A baggy top with red-hot motif does the business!

Shimmering split skirt, high boots and patterned t-shirt, Leigh-Anne's classy street look is stunning!

5 Fashion Tips...

1 Be bold – mix any colours and styles you want.

2 Slogan tops make a great statement.

3 Select the right shoes for the complete head to toe look.

4 Accessories like bracelets, rings, hairbands and crowns work wonders.

5 Be independent. You don't have to always dress like your friends.

Singing Superstars

Mega Mixin'

Some of Little Mix's biggest hits have been rearranged. Write what each song title really is.

1 GAMBA CLICK

2 RAINY COUGH FEEL

3 SET OUT MOUTH OXY

4 COUTH

5 WOPER

6 SWING

7 BAN ALL CONN

Pretend Perrie

A

B

C

D

Only one of these Perrie pictures is exactly the same as the big one. Tick the one that's NOT a pretend.

Super Search

There are 15 Little Mix words hiding in this grid. Can you spot them all?

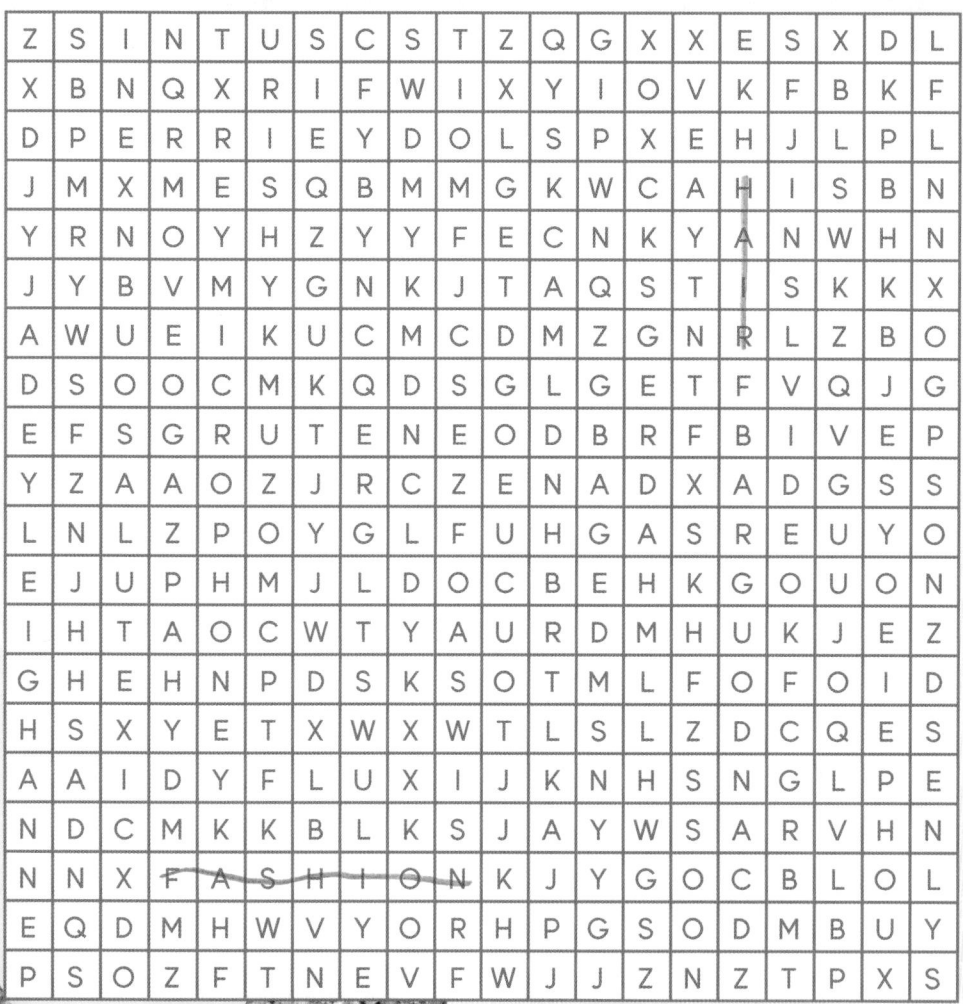

```
Z S I N T U S C S T Z Q G X X E S X D L
X B N Q X R I F W I X Y I O V K F B K F
D P E R R I E Y D O L S P X E H J L P L
J M X M E S Q B M M G K W C A H I S B N
Y R N O Y H Z Y Y F E C N K Y A N W H N
J Y B V M Y G N K J T A Q S T I S K K X
A W U E I K U C M C D M Z G N R L Z B O
D S O O C M K Q D S G L G E T F V Q J G
E F S G R U T E N E O D B R F B I V E P
Y Z A A O Z J R C Z E N A D X A D G S S
L N L Z P O Y G L F U H G A S R E U Y O
E J U P H M J L D O C B E H K G O U O N
I H T A O C W T Y A U R D M H U K J E Z
G H E H N P D S K S O T M L F O F O I D
H S X Y E T X W X W T L S L Z D C Q E S
A A I D Y F L U X I J K N H S N G L P E
N D C M K K B L K S J A Y W S A R V H N
N N X F A S H I O N K J Y G O C B L O L
E Q D M H W V Y O R H P G S O D M B U Y
P S O Z F T N E V F W J J Z N Z T P X S
```

DNA ● MICROPHONE ● PERRIE ● SONG ●

LEIGH-ANNE ● DOWNLOAD ● VIDEO ●

MOVE ● JADE ● JESY ● DANCE ●

CHART ● SALUTE ● HAIR ● FASHION ●

Quick-Fire Facts

24/12/2011

Little Mix's debut song, *Cannonball*, first went into the charts the day before Christmas!

girl power

Little Mix have four UK number one songs, but they hope to beat these numbers one day!

spice girls
9 number ones

sugababes
6 number ones

7 Colaborations

In Little Mix's 20 biggest songs they collaborated with seven other artists, including Jason Derulo, Stormzy, Sean Paul and Missy Elliott.

2012

Little Mix launched their cool collection of Primark clothes this year!

2018

This year, Little Mix revealed their third range of awesome sportswear clothing with the USA Pro label.

383 MILLION +
Number of YouTube views of the group's *Black Magic* video (May 2018).

250 MILLION +
Streams of *Shout Out To My Ex* on Spotify (May 2018).

19.7 MILLION
Amount of Instagram followers the girls have in total.

18
18 years old
Average age of the band when they first got together in 2011.

15 GCSEs
Jade is very clever, she got 15 As and A*s in her GCSE exams.

World Stars

Little Mix are global greats. Discover the stories behind their epic concerts and performances around the world.

Canada

In March 2017, Little Mix wowed fans in the Canadian cities of Toronto and Montreal. They supported Ariana Grande on her 2017 *Dangerous Woman* tour.

America

Jade, Jesy, Perrie and Leigh-Anne have sung all over the States, from Los Angeles to Las Vegas and Oklahoma to Ohio. They got the crowd really pumped up as part of Ariana Grande's tour.

Did you know?

Perrie thinks Leigh-Anne would enjoy living in Los Angeles in the future.

Did you know?

Little Mix sang at the famous Rockefeller Plaza in New York City.

Did you know?

Little Mix sang 'Love Me Like You' for the first time on the Australian X Factor.

Europe

With their *Get Weird* and *Glory Days* campaigns, Little Mix have been on stage in Germany, Italy, Spain, France, Switzerland, Sweden, Belgium, France and loads more European countries. It's fair to say that they've touched the lives of Little Mixers all over the world!

Japan

Little Mix say Japan is one of the best countries to visit. They had a bit of a scary time there though, because an earthquake struck their hotel one night!

Did you know?
The girls can sing some of 'Wings' in Japanese.

Singapore

Leigh-Anne admits that Singapore, in south east Asia, is an amazing country. The group put on a great show at the Star Theatre, with songs like *Salute* and *Secret Love Song*.

Australia

In 2016, the *Get Weird* world tour took Little Mix to Australia. They did three amazing gigs in Sydney, Melbourne and Brisbane. The following year they went back Down Under, taking the *Glory Days* tour to five Aussie cities with six concerts in total.

Did you know?
Perrie lived in New Zealand as a child. When she was on tour there she had a surprise reunion with her best friend, Mandy.

New Zealand

Little Mix journeyed to New Zealand in July 2017 to play their first concert in the country. The set list had classics like *Power*, *Black Magic* and *Hair*.

Shoe Swap

Which of these stylish shoes belongs to which singer? Draw a line to match them up.

A

C

B

D

1

3
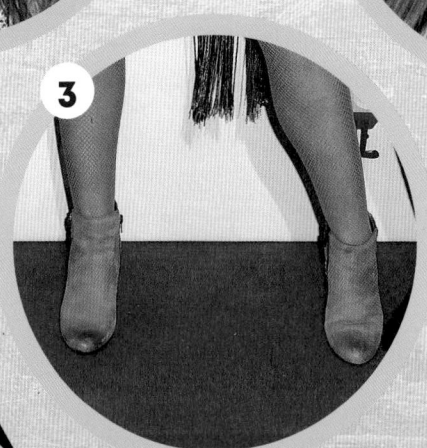

Fab fact

Some of Jade's shoes and outfits have been sold for charity.

2

4

Song or Wrong?

Which of these are real Little Mix songs and which have been made up? Tick the proper pop tunes.

- Cats & Dogs
- Electric
- Touch
- Cannonball
- Summer Song
- Wings
- Rocket Love
- Hair
- Little Me
- Move
- Black Magic
- School's Out
- Power
- Salute
- Special Secret
- Hello
- Love Me Like You

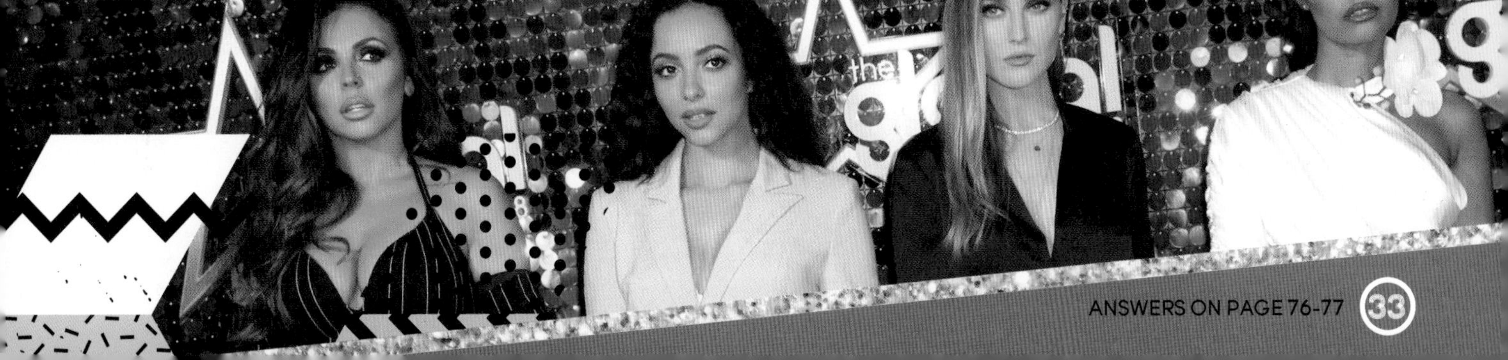

ANSWERS ON PAGE 76-77

little mix then...

>>>>>

LITTLE MIX

Wow – Little Mix have changed so much! Look back at their old style, then skip forward to their current vibe.

In 2011 and 2012, Jade wore lots of bows. Leigh-Anne's hair was mega frizzy! Perrie looked so young and fresh-faced.

Lots of curls for Jesy and Leigh-Anne. Teenage tom boy look, with socks and purple shoes!

In 2013 these simple patterns and colours looked cute!

& now!

Designer dresses and sharp hairstyles to match.
Strong make-up and powerful poses.

Modern, polished looks and careful colour coordination.

Bold, striking colours.
Girl power rules for these gals!

Camo trousers or a pretty tiara, these days Little Mix rock anything they like

11 Reasons why Little Mix Rule

Little Mix have been together since **2011**, so here are **11** reasons why they rule the pop world...

>>>>

2017

1 They have become best friends and all support and help each other. Do you want to be their BFF too?!

2 They love each other, but they also adore their supporters. They call their fantastic fans the Mixers.

3 Little Mix always have fun on stage, when they tour or make videos. Enjoying what they do is important to this group of girls!

4 The group looks stunning whenever they are on screen or in concert. Their eye-catching fashion really stands out.

5 With top songs, albums, chart success and world tours, Little Mix are pop record breakers. Remember they were the first group to win *The X Factor*!

6 Not only are they talented singers and dancers, they write bangin' songs too. Keep those lovely lyrics coming please!

7 American pop sensation Ariana Grande is a fan of Little Mix as well. Woo hoo!

8 Little Mix love puppies. Leigh-Anne has a gorgeous pug called Harvey.

9 The girls work hard and want more albums and future number ones. That's brilliant news!

10 They take cool selfies of themselves and with their fans. Being in a Little Mix photo must be crazy!

11 They launched their own Little Mix dolls, so you even get to play with the girls. Cute!

I love Little Mix because ...

Phone Fun

Time to tackle these mobile puzzles and quizzes.

Mix's Mobile

Tick which two pieces complete Jade's screensaver.

A

B

C

D

Message Mayhem

Jesy's sent Jade two messages, but some letters have changed to stars. What do you think the words are?

Hey hon! Meet at your h**se at 7pm x

Shall we all go out for d****r tomorrow night? X

Contact Clues

Perrie's phone has mixed up the names and surnames of the other Little Mix girls. Unscramble the words to reveal the proper names.

Groups
Contacts

Anne Chloe Pinking

Edith Jr Wallar

Jenny Soles

A B C D E F G H I J K L M N O P Q R S T U V W X Y Z #

10:45 AM

Contact

‹ Messages

I'm seeing my family in Essex next week.

That sounds lovely, pet. Have a smashing time!

But tonight I'm treating myself to Nandos!

Tasty. I'll be catching a train to Newcastle and then meeting me mam.

Ooh that's nice. See ya soon Poopey!

Write message ...

Send

Guess the Chat

Which two Little Mix stars are having a text chat here?

ANSWERS ON PAGE 76-77

Dancing Divas

Find your Super Fan Score!

Tick your answer to each question and discover what your Little Mix super fan score is.

>>>>>

1 How often do you listen to Little Mix songs?

At least three songs a day.
○ 10 points

Once a week.
○ 4 points

Maybe at the weekend.
○ 2 points

2 Have you seen Little Mix singing live?

No, but I have a ticket to see them.
○ 3 points

Yes I have.
○ 5 points

My dream is to see them live.
○ 2 points

3 Have you ever styled your hair to be just like them?

Definitely! I love their look.
○ 6 points

No, but that would be sick.
○ 3 points

I've done my hair AND dressed like them!
○ 10 points

4 Do you have a Little Mix poster on your bedroom wall?

I don't, but it's a great idea for my room.
○ 4 points

Yes I do.
○ 6 points

I have more than just one poster.
○ 10 points

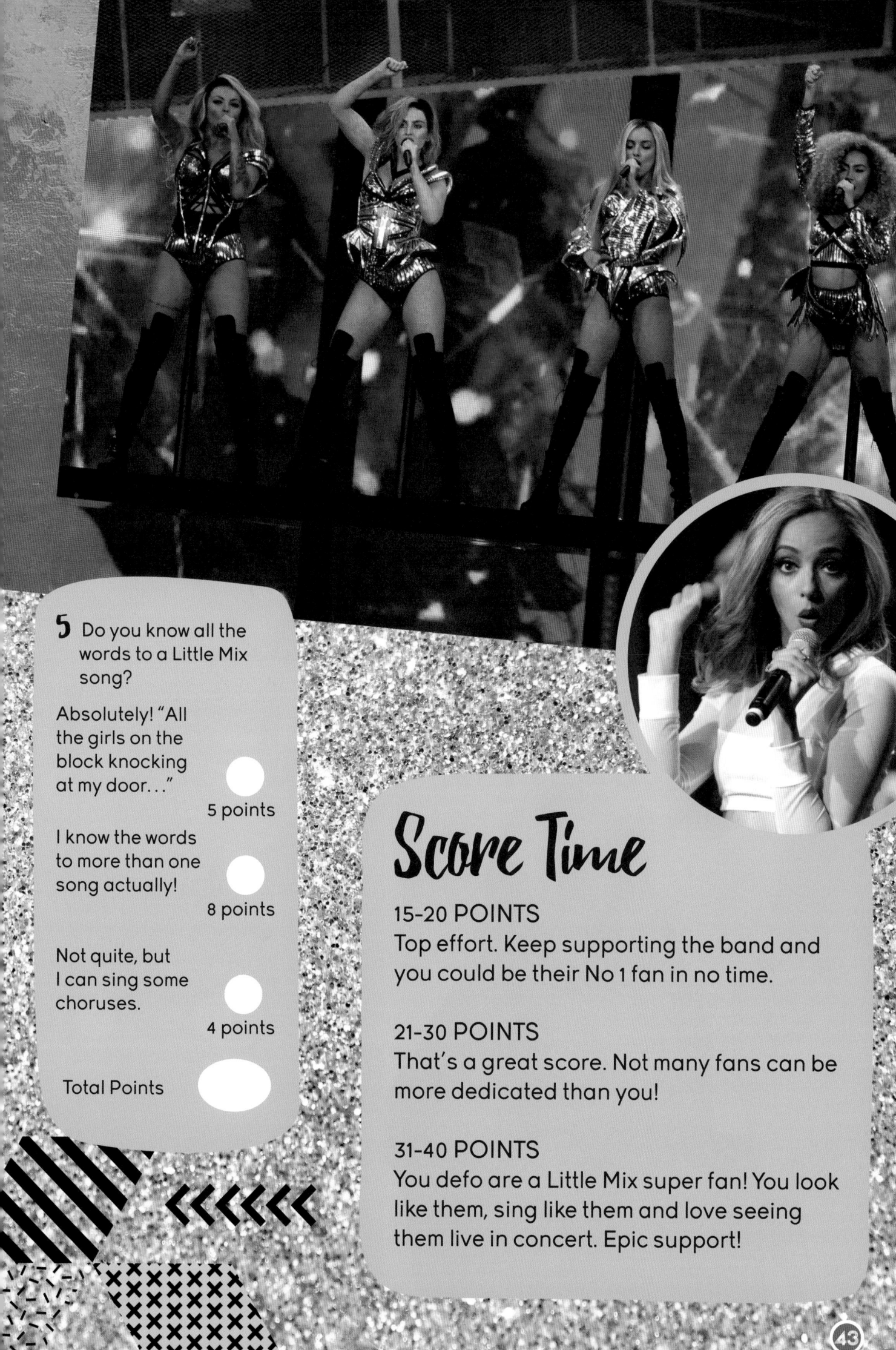

5 Do you know all the words to a Little Mix song?

Absolutely! "All the girls on the block knocking at my door…"

○ 5 points

I know the words to more than one song actually!

○ 8 points

Not quite, but I can sing some choruses.

○ 4 points

Total Points ○

Score Time

15-20 POINTS
Top effort. Keep supporting the band and you could be their No 1 fan in no time.

21-30 POINTS
That's a great score. Not many fans can be more dedicated than you!

31-40 POINTS
You defo are a Little Mix super fan! You look like them, sing like them and love seeing them live in concert. Epic support!

Fact or fiction?

1 The band used to be called Rhythmix.

Fact ◯ Fiction ◯

2 Perrie and Jade both grew up in South Shields.

Fact ◯ Fiction ◯

3 Little Mix first came together in 2011.

Fact ◯ Fiction ◯

4 They have performed for the Queen on the roof of Buckingham Palace.

Fact ◯ Fiction ◯

5 Little Mix won a Brit Award for Best British Single.

Fact ◯ Fiction ◯

95-106 CAPITAL

Decide if these Little Mix statements are a true fact or just made up nonsense!

7 Before each concert, Little Mix always eat a jam sandwich 'coz they think it brings them good luck.

Fact ⚪ Fiction ⚪

6 On a plane to Australia, the band performed a special hour-long sing along because they were bored.

Fact ⚪ Fiction ⚪

8 Jesy was a good sprint runner when she was younger.

Fact ⚪ Fiction ⚪

My fave Little Mix fact is…

Mix in the Words

These nine words will fit into the grid. Some letters are there already to help you.

DANCING
FRIENDS
CONCERT
SPECIAL
YOUTUBE
AWARDS
FUN
SINGING
GROUP

Faces in the crowd

Leigh-Anne, Jesy, Jade and Perrie are hiding in this Little Mix concert crowd. Circle them all.

Fun fact

Jesy often gives the girls a pep talk before they go on stage, to help them feel less nervous.

Best Fests!

The girls love singing and performing at massive music festivals. Here are Little Mix's best fest photos.

Put your shades and sunglasses on, here they are at the British Summertime Festival in Hyde Park!

Festival fact

Sadly Perrie was unwell at the iHeartRadio Festival, but Jade, Jesy and Leigh-Anne put on a fantastic show!

In sunny Las Vegas in America, Little Mix wowed the crowds with songs like *Touch* and *Wings*.

At the awesome T in the Park fest in Scotland, Jade jumped around in these flashy tartan trousers. Great look!

Jesy really enjoyed strutting it at the V Festival because it was in her home county of Essex!

Festival fact

Jesy said V Festival was one of the best concerts they ever played!

Festival fact

Little Mix first appeared at the Radio 1's Big Weekend in Northern Ireland back in 2013.

At Radio 1's Big Weekend in 2017, Little Mix's set list included *Power, Black Magic, Salute* and *Wings*. The crowd in Hull went crazy!

Little Mix have twice rocked the Apple Music Festival in London.

a-Maze-ing

Enter here!

Help the four girls get through
the maze to the centre. Check out
the 'a-maze-ing' facts in the middle too!

Jade
is very pretty,
but she was stood up at
her school prom. Poor thing!

If Leigh-Anne had to change her
name to a food, she says she'd be
called Leigh-Anne Lasagne!

If Jesy had a super power she'd
like to click her fingers and
instantly be anywhere she
liked.

Create Cool Clothes

Here's your chance to design new clothes for Little Mix. Get your colourful pens and pencils out and start creating a cool look!

Draw some shoes, bags and hair accessories too!

Bags

Fab fact

Leigh-Anne loves posh designer clothes by Louis Vuitton and cute Chanel bags.

Hair Accessories

Shoes

Little Differences

Eye See You!

The photographer has zoomed in on Little Mix's eyes.

Which pair belongs to which singer?

1

2

3

Fab fact

One of Perrie's fave make-ups is eye mascara.

4

ANSWERS ON PAGE 76-77

Fab Friends

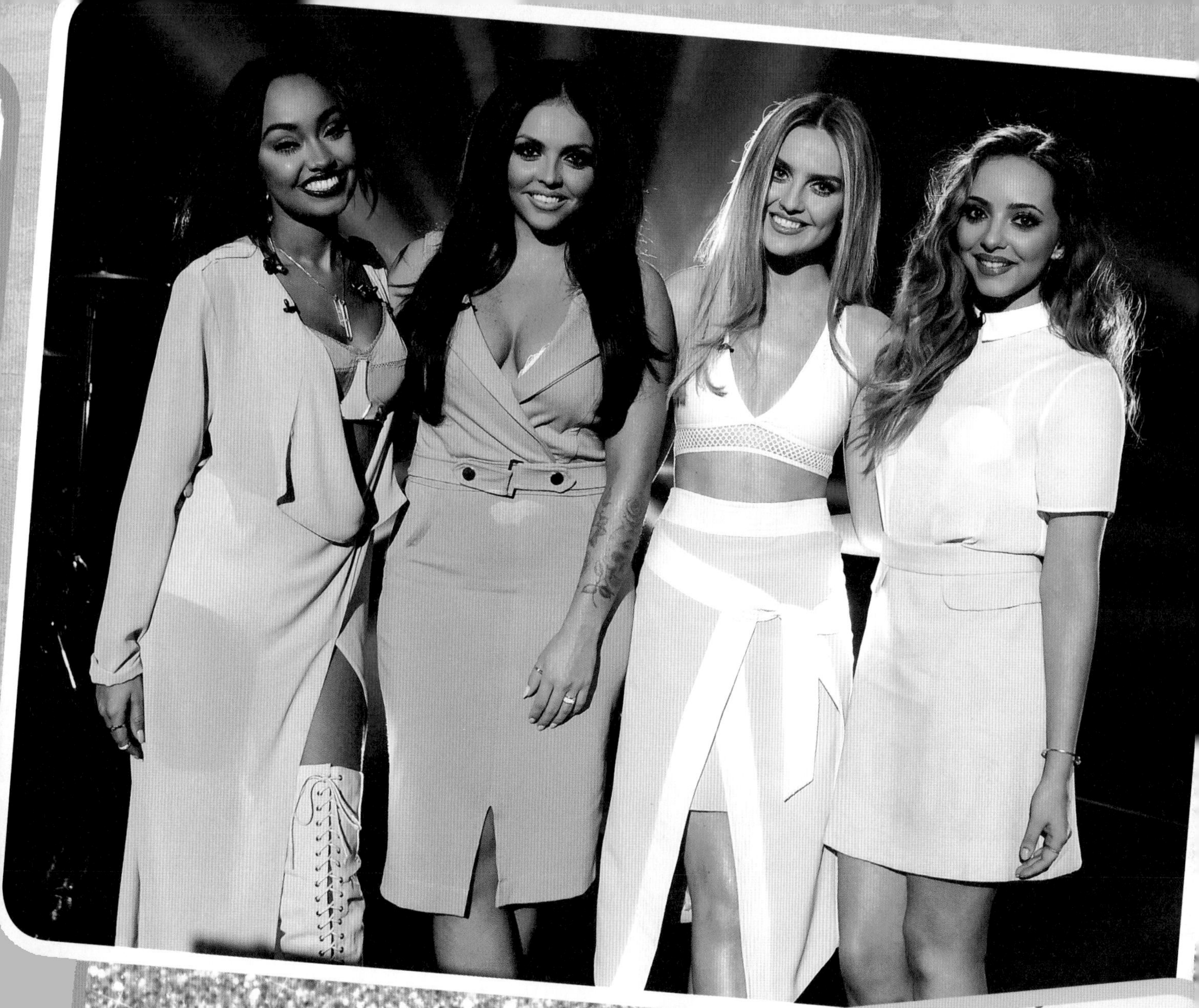

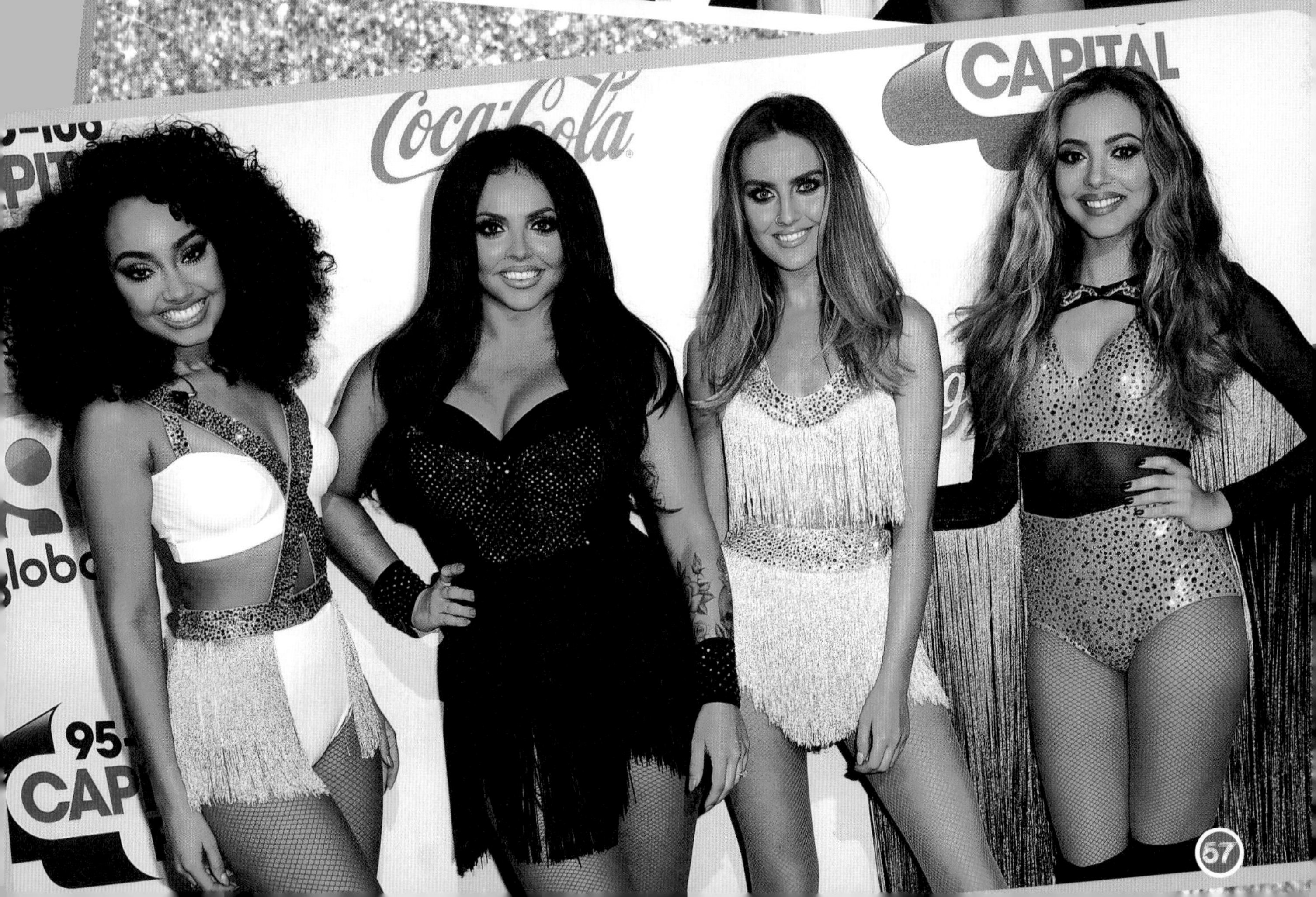
Coca-Cola
CAPITAL

Live the Little Mix Life!

Wanna be like your fave stars? Check out these top tips to help you live the Little Mix way!

Be Strong

Not physically, but strong in your mind and how you think about yourself. Some people have said mean things about Little Mix, but they just ignore any nasty chat and enjoy their singing and performing.

Be Healthy

Little Mix enjoy having an active lifestyle, with plenty of exercise from their dance routines and rehearsals. They like to eat a healthy and balanced diet too, but they also treat themselves to yummy things like cake!

Be Glamourous

The girls are great at getting glammed up to the max! With amazing hairstyles, lush make-up and fun outfits, Jesy, Perrie, Jade and Leigh-Anne know how to turn on the style when they meet their fans.

Be Generous

Little Mix earn lots of money, but they look after their friends and family too. Jade bought her mum a car for Christmas and splashed out on a family trip to Disneyland! You can be generous in other ways and help people close to you.

Be Famous

Obviously if you're going to be in the world's biggest girl group, you're going to be mega famous! Your phone will be full of celebrity friends and messages and you'll live the red carpet life.

Be a Prankster

Little Mix enjoy a giggle and a practical joke. They've pretended to storm out of TV and radio interviews, talked in silly accents and made prank calls to celebs like Taylor Swift and James Corden! What fun jokes can you play?

Be Nice

Yep, it's important to be nice to your friends, family and the people you meet. Little Mix tour the world, chatting with people from all walks of life. They also support charities like Children In Need.

Spooky Shapes

Little Mix are hiding in the dark! Work out which spooky outline belongs to which star.

1

2

3

4

Frightening fact

Leigh-Anne and Jesy's fave scary music is the classic pop track 'Thriller' by Michael Jackson.

Singer Scramble

Which two Little Mix singers are scrambled up in this grid?

Ssshhh!

Do you know these funny secrets and giggles about Little Mix?

American rapper Missy Elliott is their dream fifth member of the band!

Jade bakes a lot and makes really tasty brownies!

Perrie loves the cheesy 1990s American TV show Saved By The Bell!

Jesy likes to eat Easter eggs when it's not even Easter!

Their mums have a 'Mummy Mixers' Whatsapp chat group together!

Leigh-Anne had a Justin Bieber poster on her bedroom wall!

On National Wear Your Pyjamas to Work Day, Jesy and Jade dressed in matching Toy Story pyjamas!

Leigh-Anne would love to skydive!

At first the girls didn't like the band name Little Mix, but they soon grew to love it!

Jesy's parents are John and Janice. She has brothers called Joseph and Jonathan, and a sister Jade. Lots of Js!

Jesy used to enjoy the 100-metre sprint race, but the starting pistol scared her too much!

When she was younger, Perrie once tasted a dog biscuit!

Awesome Awards

With their super songs and dazzling dances, Little Mix have enjoyed lots of success and won many trophies over the years.

Going Global
Little Mix were big news at the Global Awards 2018. Jesy and the girls walked off with Best Group, Best Song (*Power*) and Best British Artist. Three awards in one night isn't bad, hey?

MTV Mania
Little Mix have two MTV Europe Music Awards to show off. In 2017 and 2015 they took top spot in the Best UK & Ireland Act. Trophy-tastic!

Big Brits
So far, the biggest and best award the girls have is their Brit Award in 2017. They won Best British Single with *Shout Out To My Ex* and were over the moon to win!

Top Teens
Fans have twice voted Little Mix as winners in Radio 1's Teen Awards and the Teen Choice Awards in America.

Award extra

Little Mix's first performance at the Brits was in 2016 with *Black Magic*.

Glamour Girls

The band first attended the Glamour Awards in 2012. Since then, the fearsome foursome have scooped three prizes – twice landing Best Music Act and also Best Band.

Your Little Mix Award

Here you can draw a trophy that you'd award to Little Mix. Write why they deserve it, too!

Little Mix won this award for . . . .

Pop Poster

Create your own Little Mix tour poster. Draw the girls, add a tour name – you could even include your home town as one of the venues!

Fill this box with your sick design.

Shout Out to My X

Perrie is desperately trying to find her way to the big X in the centre. Draw a path to it from the start point.

Easy as A,B,C!

Bust out all your Little Mix knowledge and choose A, B, or C to these quick questions.

1 Which year did they win *The X Factor*?

A 2009
B 2010
C 2011

2 What was the second song the girls released?

A *Wings*
B *Cannonball*
C *Move*

3 Which of the girls once took a bite of a dog biscuit?

A Leigh-Anne
B Jesy
C Perrie

4 Can you name the album that's been in the top 40 for over 70 weeks?

A *DNA*
B *Get Weird*
C *Glory Days*

5 How many weeks was *Black Magic* number 1 in the UK charts?

A Three Weeks
B One Week
C Six Weeks

6 Who has the nickname Pez?

A Jade
B Perrie
C Leigh-Anne

7 Who celebrates their birthday on Boxing Day?

A Jesy
B Jade
C Perrie

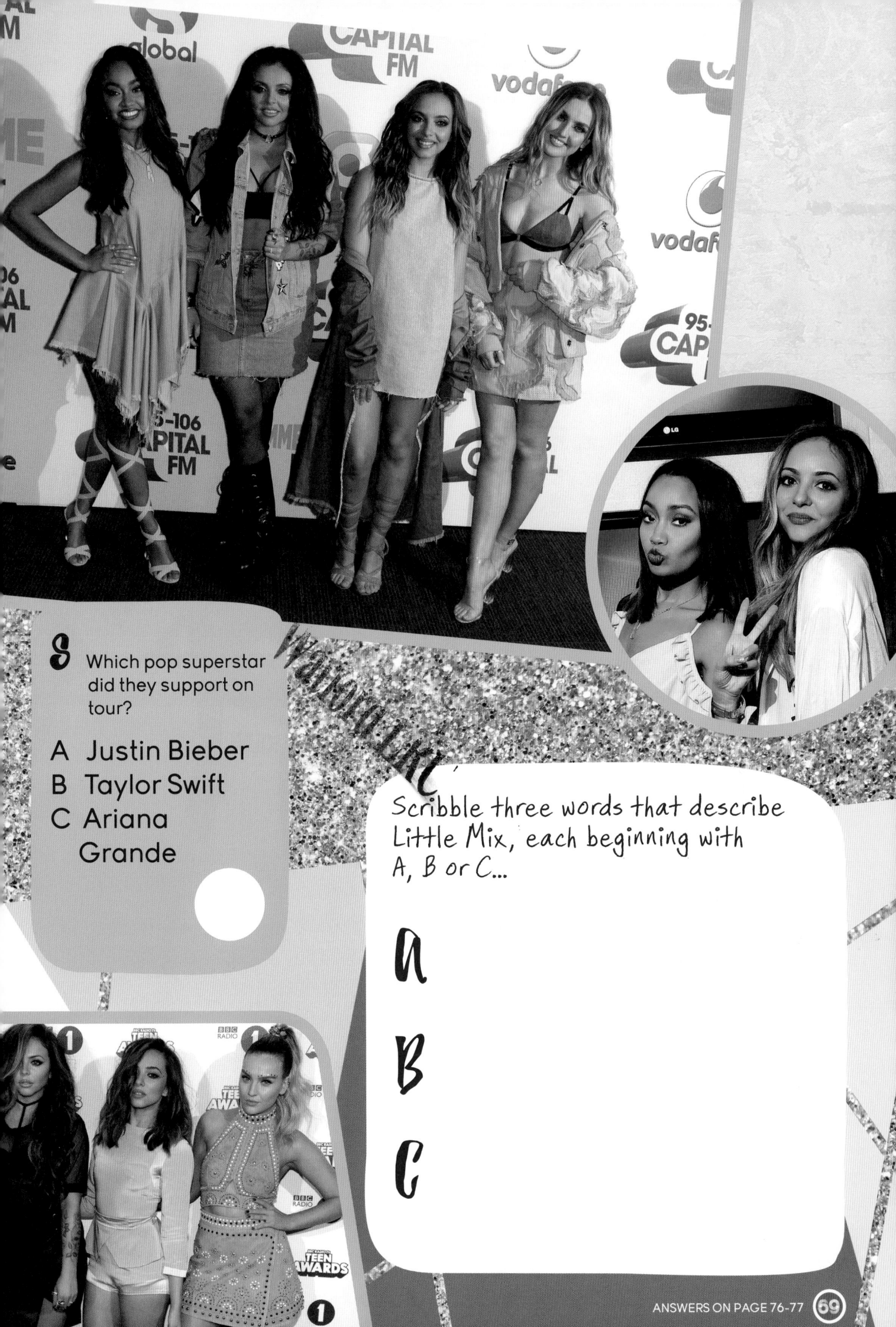

S Which pop superstar did they support on tour?

A Justin Bieber
B Taylor Swift
C Ariana Grande

Scribble three words that describe Little Mix, each beginning with A, B or C...

A

B

C

Pop Princesses

Sunny Days

Little Mix are lovin' the sunshine today, but can you work out who are behind the silly sunny objects?

1

2

3

4

Little Mix
Memories

Take a close look at the pictures below for 60 seconds, then turn the page to answer ten tricky questions about what you've seen...

Turn over for the test!

73

Little Mix Memories

See what you can remember from the pictures on the previous page.

1 How many pink microphones were shown?

5 How many lipsticks were there?

2 What colour was Jade's dress?

6 What was over Jesy's right eye?

3 Which comic character was Jesy standing with?

7 Which Little Mix was wearing a poppy on her dress?

4 Who was holding a colourful handbag?

8 What was the number on Jesy's t-shirt?

ANSWERS ON PAGE 76-77

2019 Predictions

just for fun!

It'll be a miracle if these funny things happen to Little Mix in 2019 – but let's hope they do!

Little Mix team up with the Spice Girls, their fave UK girl group!

Jade signs for Newcastle United, her fave football team!

The stylish girls model at the New York, Paris and Milan Fashion Weeks!

They enter The X Factor again... and win!

They make a Little Mix movie and it's a smash hit!

Their new album is number one all year – that's 52 weeks in a row!

73

Quiz Answers

Page 18
GUESS WHO?:
1. Jesy; 2. Perrie; 3. Perrie & Jesy; 4. Perrie; 5. Leigh-Anne; 6. Perrie; 7. Leigh-Anne; 8. Jade; 9. Leigh-Anne.

Page 19
LITTLE MIXED-UP
Jesy:
Chest D; Legs C; Shoes D
Leigh-Anne:
Chest C; Legs A; Shoes B
Perrie:
Chest A; Legs B; Shoes A
Jade:
Chest B; Legs D; Shoes C

Page 26
MEGA MIXIN':
1. Black Magic;
2. Change Your Life;
3. Shout Out to my Ex;
4. Touch; 5. Power;
6. Wings; 7. Cannonball

Page 27
PRETEND PERRIE: C

Page 28
SUPER SEARCH:

Z	S	I	N	T	U	S	C	S	T	Z	Q	G	X	X	E	S	X	D	L
X	B	N	Q	X	R	I	F	W	I	X	Y	I	O	V	K	F	B	K	F
D	P	E	R	R	I	E	Y	D	O	L	S	P	X	E	H	J	L	P	L
J	M	X	M	E	S	Q	B	M	M	G	K	W	C	A	H	I	S	B	N
Y	R	N	O	Y	H	Z	Y	Y	F	E	C	N	K	Y	A	N	W	H	N
J	Y	B	V	M	Y	G	N	K	J	T	A	Q	S	T	I	S	K	K	X
A	W	U	E	I	K	U	C	M	C	D	M	Z	G	N	R	L	Z	B	O
D	S	O	O	C	M	K	Q	D	S	G	L	G	E	T	F	V	Q	J	G
E	F	S	G	R	U	T	E	N	E	O	D	B	R	F	B	I	V	E	P
Y	Z	A	A	O	Z	J	R	C	Z	E	N	A	D	X	A	D	G	S	S
L	N	L	Z	P	O	Y	G	L	F	U	H	G	A	S	R	E	U	Y	O
E	J	U	P	H	M	J	L	D	O	C	B	E	H	K	G	O	U	O	N
I	H	T	A	O	C	W	T	Y	A	U	R	D	M	H	U	K	J	E	Z
G	H	E	H	N	P	D	S	K	S	O	T	M	L	F	O	F	O	I	D
H	S	X	Y	E	T	X	W	X	W	T	L	S	L	Z	D	C	Q	E	S
A	A	I	D	Y	F	L	U	X	I	J	K	N	H	S	N	G	L	P	E
N	D	C	M	K	K	B	L	K	S	J	A	Y	W	S	A	R	V	H	N
N	N	X	F	A	S	H	I	O	N	K	J	Y	G	O	C	B	L	O	L
E	Q	D	M	H	W	V	Y	O	R	H	P	G	S	O	D	M	B	U	Y
P	S	O	Z	F	T	N	E	V	F	W	J	J	Z	N	Z	T	P	X	S

Page 32
SHOE SWAP:
A4; B3; C2; D1

Page 33
SONG OR WRONG?
*Wings, Power, Black Magic,
Salute,
Touch,
Cannonball,
Move,
Little Me,
Hair*
and
*Love Me
Like You*
are all real
Little Mix
songs.

Pages 38-39
PHONE FUN:

Mix's Mobile:
Pieces C and D

Message Mayhem:
house & dinner

Contact Clues:
Anne Chloe Pinking =
Leigh-Anne Pinnock

Edith Jr Waller =
Jade Thirlwall

Jenny Soles =
Jesy Nelson

Guess The Chat:
Jesy and Jade

Pages 44-45
FACT OR FICTION?
1. Fact; 2. Fact
3. Fact; 4. Fiction
5. Fact; 6. Fiction
7. Fiction; 8. Fact

Page 46
MIX IN THE WORDS:

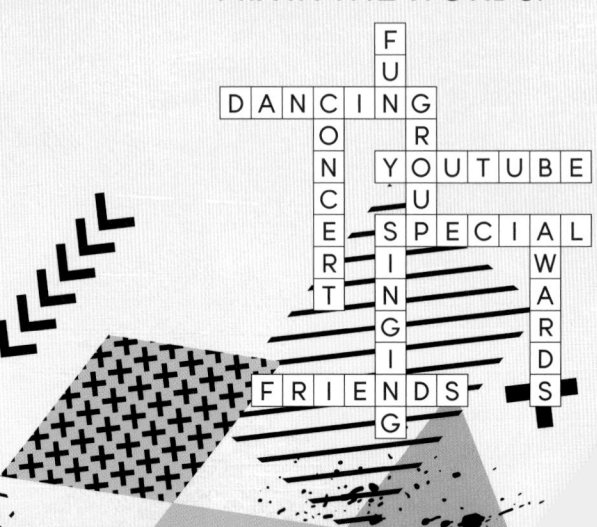

Picture Credits

Cover
Front - Doug Peters/Doug Peters/EMPICS
Entertainment
Ian West/PA Archive/PA Images
Back - Ian West/PA Archive/PA Images

Pages
6-7
Marcel Thomas/Zuma Press/PA Images
AFLO/AFLO/Press Association Images
Chris J. Ratcliffe/PA Archive/PA Images

8-9
Doug Peters/Doug Peters/EMPICS
Entertainment
Martin Rickett/PA Archive/PA Images
Matt Crossick/Matt Crossick/Empics
Entertainment
Simone Comi/IPA MilestoneMedia/PA Images

10-11
JPA/AFF/PA Images
Yui Mok/PA Archive/PA Images
Ian West/PA Archive/PA Images

12-13
JPA/AFF/PA Images
Isabel Infantes/PA Wire/PA Images
AJM/EMPICS Entertainment

14-15
© AFF-USA.COM/AFF/PA Images
AFLO/AFLO/Press Association Images
AJM/EMPICS Entertainment

16-17
Ian West/PA Wire/PA Images
© AFF-USA.COM/AFF/PA Images
Doug Peters/Doug Peters/EMPICS
Entertainment

18-19
John Phillips/EMPICS Entertainment
Doug Peters/Doug Peters/EMPICS
Entertainment
Ian West/PA Archive/PA Images

20-21
© AFF-USA.COM/AFF/PA Images

22-23
Daniel Leal-Olivas/PA Archive/PA Images
Martin Hangen/Imago/PA Images
Doug Peters/Doug Peters/EMPICS
Entertainment
Yui Mok/PA Archive/PA Images
Katja Ogrin/EMPICS Entertainment/EMPICS
Entertainment
John Phillips/EMPICS Entertainment

24-25
Daniel Leal-Olivas/PA Archive/PA Images
JAMES ATOA/UPI/PA Images
Doug Peters/Doug Peters/EMPICS
Entertainment
Ryan Phillips/PA Archive/PA Images
Owen Humphreys/PA Archive/PA Images
Matt Crossick/Matt Crossick/Empics
Entertainment

26-27
Doug Peters/Doug Peters/EMPICS
Entertainment
Daniel Leal-Olivas/PA Archive/PA Images
Matt Crossick/Matt Crossick/Empics
Entertainment

28-29
Matt Crossick/Matt Crossick/Empics
Entertainment
Owen Humphreys/PA Archive/PA Images
Matt Crossick/Matt Crossick/Empics
Entertainment
John Mather/EMPICS Entertainment
Doug Peters/allaction.co.uk /EMPICS
Entertainment

30-31
John Barrett/Zuma Press/PA Images
Marcel Thomas/Zuma Press/PA Images
AFLO/AFLO/Press Association Images
Aaron Chown/PA Archive/PA Images

32-33
Ian West/PA Archive/PA Images
Isabel Infantes/PA Wire/PA Images

34-35
Suzan Moore/EMPICS Entertainment
Yui Mok/PA Archive/PA Images
Hubert Boesl/DPA/PA Images
Isabel Infantes/PA Wire/PA Images
Doug Peters/Doug Peters/EMPICS
Entertainment
JPA/AFF/PA Images

36-37
Frantzesco Kangaris/PA Archive/PA Images
Matt Crossick/Matt Crossick/Empics
Entertainment
© AFF-USA.COM/AFF/PA Images
Dave Bedrosian/Geisler-Fotopress/DPA/PA
Images
Daniel Leal-Olivas/PA Archive/PA Images
Chris Radburn/PA Archive/PA Images

38-39
Ian West/PA Archive/PA Images
Joel Ryan/PA Wire/PA Images

40-41
Yui Mok/PA Archive/PA Images
Chris J. Ratcliffe/PA Archive/PA Images
PictureGroup/SIPA USA/PA Images
JPA/AFF/PA Images
Chris J. Ratcliffe/PA Archive/PA Images
Danny Lawson/PA Archive/PA Images

42-43
Audrey Poree/ABACA/PA Images
Matt Crossick/Matt Crossick/Empics
Entertainment
Charles Guerin/ABACA USA/PA Images

44-45
Ian West/PA Archive/PA Images
Andrew Parsons/Sunday Times/PA Wire/PA
Images
Yui Mok/PA Archive/PA Images

46-47
Ian West/PA Archive/PA Images
Roberto Finizio/Zuma Press/PA Images

48-49
Suzan Moore/EMPICS Entertainment
AJM/EMPICS Entertainment
Andrew Milligan/PA Archive/PA Images
Daniel Leal-Olivas/PA Archive/PA Images
PA/PA Archive/PA Images

50-51
Chris J. Ratcliffe/PA Archive/PA Images
Doug Peters/Doug Peters/EMPICS
Entertainment

52-53
Isabel Infantes/PA Wire/PA Images

54-55
Dan Law/PA Archive/PA Images
Daniel Leal-Olivas/PA Archive/PA Images
Ian West/PA Archive/PA Images
Doug Peters/Doug Peters/EMPICS
Entertainment
JPA/AFF/PA Images

56-57
Ian West/PA Archive/PA Images
Doug Peters/Doug Peters/EMPICS
Entertainment

58-59
Doug Peters/Doug Peters/EMPICS
Entertainment
Daniel Leal-Olivas/PA Archive/PA Images

60-61
JPA/AFF/PA Images

62-63
Ryan Phillips/PA Archive/PA Images
Ian West/PA Archive/PA Images

64-65
Isabel Infantes/PA Wire/PA Images
Ian West/PA Archive/PA Images
Matt Crossick/Matt Crossick/Empics
Entertainment
Ian West/PA Archive/PA Images

66-67
© AFF-USA.COM/AFF/PA Images
Doug Peters/Doug Peters/EMPICS
Entertainment

68-69
Doug Peters/Doug Peters/EMPICS
Entertainment
Ian West/PA Archive/PA Images
Matt Crossick/PA Archive/PA Images

70-71
Ian West/PA Archive/PA Images
Doug Peters/Doug Peters/EMPICS
Entertainment

72-73
AFLO/AFLO/Press Association Images
Ian West/PA Archive/PA Images
David Jensen/EMPICS Entertainment
Doug Peters/Doug Peters/EMPICS
Entertainment
Chris Radburn/PA Archive/PA Images
Suzan Moore/EMPICS Entertainment
Ian West/PA Archive/PA Images

74-75
AFLO/AFLO/Press Association Images
Ian West/PA Archive/PA Images
Doug Peters/Doug Peters/EMPICS
Entertainment
Daniel Leal-Olivas/PA Archive/PA Images
Ian West/PA Archive/PA Images

76-77
Roberto Finizio/Zuma Press/PA Images
Dan Law/PA Archive/PA Images